D0899784

Practice Test for the Cognitive Abilities Test (CogAT®*)

Multilevel Edition (Levels A – H)

By Mercer Publishing

Practice Test for the

Cognitive Abilities Test (CogAT®*)

Multilevel Edition (Levels A – H)

A study aid to help your child get into a gifted program.

Mercer Publishing

INTRODUCTION

As a parent and educator, I understand how important it is to ensure your children are given the opportunites they deserve when it comes to their education. One of the greatest opportunities your child will have is enterring the gifted program, if they can qualify for the program based on their test scores.

One of the primary tools for measuring a student's ability to enter the gifted program is the Cognitive Abilities Test (CogAT®*) published by Riverside Publishing. This test is made up of tests in three areas: Verbal, Quantitative and Nonverbal. Your child's score on this test is likely the sole predictor of their inclusion, or non-inclusion, into the gifted program.

Most resources state that there are really no ways to prepare for this test - that your child should only get a good night's sleep before taking the test. An official practice test with sample questions does exist, but it is only available to licensed test administrators. It is guaranteed that if your child is not familiar with some of the symbols used in the test or if they have never done some of the types of problems before, that they will not do as well as they could on this test – perhaps jepordizing their admission into the gifted program. So what should the average parent do?

If you have purchased this practice test, you have taken the first step. This practice test contains nine tests in the three test areas found on the CogAT®* Multilevel Edition (levels A – H), which is usually given to students in second grade and above:

VERBAL

Verbal Classification	20 questions
Sentence Completion	20 questions
Verbal Analogies	25 questions

QUANTITATIVE

Quantitative Relations	25 questions
Number Series	20 questions
Equation Building	15 questions

NONVERBAL

Figure Classification	25 questions
Figure Analogies	25 questions
Figure Analysis	15 questions

The object of this practice test is to familiarize your child with the types of questions they will face on test day, how the tests are formatted, the symbols used and the number of questions in in each test area. However, since this practice test has not been standardized with Riverside Publishing and the actual CogAT®* test, a valid CogAT®* test score cannot be concluded from their results on this practice test.

Good luck on this practice test and your upcoming gifted program test.

Mercer Publishing

* CogAT® is a registered trademark of Houghton Mifflin Company, which was not involved in the production of, and does not endorse, this practice test.

TABLE OF CONTENTS

TEST TAKING INFORMATION

The Cognitive Abilities Test (CogAT®*) Multilevel Edition, which is usually given to students in second grade and above, is a timed, multiple choice test. The test is self-administered, where the student reads and answers the questions themselves. Most testing for the CogAT®* Multilevel Edition is done using electronically scored answer sheets, although answering in hand-scored booklets is sometimes also done.

The official guideline from the publisher is that students should not guess if they do not know the answer – that random guessing compromises the validity of the scores. However, the CogAT®* score is calculated based on the number of right answers and the student is not penalized for incorrect answers. As a parent looking for a high score, it is better for your child to answer all questions than leave an answer blank.

There are some approaches to standardized testing that have been proven to increase test scores. Review the following strategies with your child and have them practice these as they go through the practice test.

Listen Carefully. Instructions will be given to your child during the exam, including directions for each section and how to fill out the test forms. Many errors are made because children do not listen to the instructions as carefully as they should. If your child fills in the answers incorrectly or marks in the wrong section, your child's score will be lowered significantly.

Read the Entire Question. Some children begin filling in answers before they finish reading the entire question. It could be that the last part of the question has the information needed to answer the question correctly.

Look at all the Available Answers. In their desire to finish quickly or first, many children select the first answer that seems right to them without reading all of the answers and choosing the one that best answers the question. No additional points are given for finishing the test early. Make sure your child understands the importance of evaluating all the answers before choosing one.

Skip Difficult Questions – Return to Them Later. Many children will sit and worry about a hard question, spending so much time on one problem that they never get to problems that they would be able to answer correctly if they only had enough time. Explain to your child that they can always return to a difficult question once they finish the test section.

Eliminate Answer Choices. If your child can eliminate one or more of the answer choices as definitely wrong, their chances of guessing correctly among the remaining choices improve their odds of getting the answer right.

Practice Filling Out a Bubble Test Form. Many errors are made on the CogAT®* exam because the students do not know how to fill out a bubble test form. A sample test form has been included in Appendix A. Have your child practice filling in answers in the bubbles in the sample form so they will know what to expect on the exam day.

Now, on to the practice test.

VERBAL CLASSIFICATION

Each question in this section contains three words in bold letters. Review these words and determine why they are similar. Select the word from the five available answers that is most similar to the bold words.

20 questions
Approximate time to complete: 10 minutes

1. **yellow   purple   green**
   a. caterpillar   b. brown   c. chalk   d. pretty   e. colorful

2. **apple   orange   cantaloupe**
   a. banana   b. fruit   c. carrot   d. vegetable   e. candy

3. **lake   stream   pond**
   a. marina   b. fish   c. boat   d. ocean   e. swim

4. **milk   coffee   juice**
   a. lemonade   b. drink   c. snack   d. cup   e. thirsty

5. **mother   father   daughter**
   a. boy   b. family   c. happy   d. group   e. son

6. **furious   angry   irate**
   a. calm   b. pleasant   c. mad   d. body   e. work

7. **sun   lemon   daffodil**
   a. grapes   b. rain   c. smiles   d. beautiful   e. banana

8. **nice   helpful   polite**
   a. careful   b. respectful   c. picky   d. pretty   e. fancy

9. **cup   pint   quart**
    a. measure   b. gallon   c. pound   d. pour   e. mix

10. **almond   pecan   peanut**
    a. nut   b. butter   c. food   d. walnut   e. tree

11. **sunny   rainy   snowy**
    a. cloudy   b. winter   c. cold   d. happy   e. weather

12. **robin   sparrow   eagle**
    a. flying   b. airplane   c. bird   d. hawk   e. nest

13. **triangle   diamond   oval**
    a. ball   b. circle   c. shape   d. baseball   e. character

14. **orbit   circle   ring**
    a. round   b. jewelry   c. pretty   d. square   e. shape

15. **cut   slice   tear**
    a. rip   b. knife   c. scissors   d. damage   e. nature

16. **roof   window   wall**
    a. house   b. apartment   c. door   d. car   e. shed

17. **bake   grill   roast**
    a. food   b. kitchen   c. fry   d. hungry   e. eat

18. **fish   submarine   scubadiver**
    a. boat   b. shark   c. vacation   d. swim   e. ocean

19. **hour   month   week**
    a. second   b. time   c. calendar   d. work   e. schedule

20. truck   bicycle   wheelbarrow
    a. fast   b. motor   c. car   d. highway   e. drive

SENTENCE COMPLETION

Each sentence in this section is missing a word. Select the word from the five available answers that best completes the sentence.

20 questions
Approximate time to complete: 10 minutes

1. **He spent so much money on the toy that his piggybank was**
   _____ .
   a. full   b. empty   c. tired   d. wealthy   e. hungry

2. **When four year old Michael _____ up, he wants to be a fireman.**
   a. rests   b. throws   c. grows   d. tires   e. cheers

3. **The dog _____ at the delivery man.**
   a. mooed   b. meowed   c. yelled   d. frowned   e. barked

4. **Matthew stood by the mailbox, waiting for the mailman to deliver the _____ he was expecting.**
   a. baby   b. letter   c. flowers   d. message   e. present

5. **When they realized the checker piece was missing, they went to _____ for it.**
   a. check   b. game   c. look   d. fight   e. play

6. **To open the door, he put the key in the _____ and turned it.**
   a. keyring   b. lock   c. house   d. door   e. window

7. **It is raining outside so I should remember to take my _____ so I don't get wet.**
   a. umbrella   b. sunglasses   c. skis   d. shorts   e. hat

8. The brothers worked together, _____ each other to pick up the toys.
   a. avoiding   b. harming   c. helping   d. laughing   e. delaying

9. They enjoyed the rollercoaster so much, they stood in line to go on the _____ again.
   a. bathroom   b. ride   c. seat   d. fair   e. carnival

10. She kept the secret, not sharing it with anyone, just like she _____.
    a. threatened   b. shared   c. hid   d. smiled   e. promised

11. Both bananas and oranges have a _____ .
    a. party   b. food   c. peel   d. fruit   e. snack

12. John is my best friend and I _____ him very much.
    a. like   b. avoid   c. cheat   d. hurt   e. annoy

13. When we heard school was closed because of too much _____, we hurried to get our sleds.
    a. sun   b. rain   c. homework   d. snow   e. time

14. Ice cream _____ if it doesn't stay cold.
    a. tires   b. melts   c. licks   d. freezes   e. enjoys

15. Holly is so smart. She gets done with her work _____ than the other kids in the class.
    a. slower   b. further   c. smaller   d. neater   e. faster

16. Claire was in such a hurry because she was _____ for her meeting.
    a. tired   b. early   c. late   d. surprised   e. prepared

17. Oranges _____ on trees.
    a. flower   b. grow   c. peel   d. work   e. pick

18. **I am saving the cookies for the party, so please don't _____ them.**
    a. keep   b. bake   c. eat   d. save   e. drink

19. **She was surprised when the little boy laughed after hearing such a _____ story.**
    a. happy   b. funny   c. long   d. open   e. sad

20. **My grandmother is my mother's _____.**
    a. sister   b. daughter   c. father   d. mother   e. son

VERBAL ANALOGIES

Each question in this section contains three words in bold letters. Review the first two words and determine how they are related. Select the word from the five available answers that has the same relationship with the third word.

25 questions
Approximate time to complete: 10 minutes

1. **big** ⟶ **biggest : small** ⟶
   a. tiny   b. smallest   c. elfin   d. weak   e. young

2. **train** ⟶ **engineer : plane** ⟶
   a. horse   b. airport   c. passenger   d. pilot   e. flight

3. **pea** ⟶ **pod : banana** ⟶
   a. monkey   b. yellow   c. butter   d. fruit   e. peel

4. **sick** ⟶ **healthy : poor** ⟶
   a. money   b. wealthy   c. poverty   d. injured   e. happy

5. **baseball** ⟶ **mitt : fish** ⟶
   a. bat   b. hook   c. boots   d. aquarium   e. crab

6. **stove** ⟶ **kitchen : bathtub** ⟶
   a. sink   b. bedroom   c. refrigerator   d. clean   e. bathroom

7. **finger** ⟶ **hand : toe** ⟶
   a. foot   b. polish   c. toenail   d. leg   e. ankle

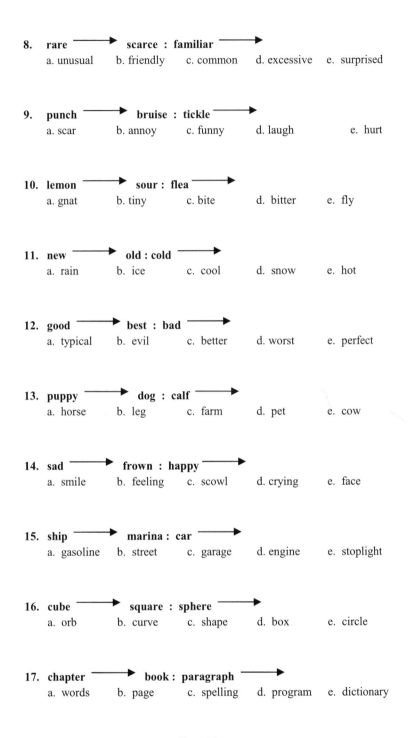

8. **rare** ——▶ **scarce : familiar** ——▶
    a. unusual   b. friendly   c. common   d. excessive   e. surprised

9. **punch** ——▶ **bruise : tickle** ——▶
    a. scar   b. annoy   c. funny   d. laugh   e. hurt

10. **lemon** ——▶ **sour : flea** ——▶
    a. gnat   b. tiny   c. bite   d. bitter   e. fly

11. **new** ——▶ **old : cold** ——▶
    a. rain   b. ice   c. cool   d. snow   e. hot

12. **good** ——▶ **best : bad** ——▶
    a. typical   b. evil   c. better   d. worst   e. perfect

13. **puppy** ——▶ **dog : calf** ——▶
    a. horse   b. leg   c. farm   d. pet   e. cow

14. **sad** ——▶ **frown : happy** ——▶
    a. smile   b. feeling   c. scowl   d. crying   e. face

15. **ship** ——▶ **marina : car** ——▶
    a. gasoline   b. street   c. garage   d. engine   e. stoplight

16. **cube** ——▶ **square : sphere** ——▶
    a. orb   b. curve   c. shape   d. box   e. circle

17. **chapter** ——▶ **book : paragraph** ——▶
    a. words   b. page   c. spelling   d. program   e. dictionary

18. **brush** ⟶ **hair : mop** ⟶
    a. wash   b. vacuum   c. floor   d. wipe   e. house

19. **apple** ⟶ **banana : carrot** ⟶
    a. grape   b. broccoli   c. grain   d. dinner   e. rabbit

20. **college** ⟶ **university : market** ⟶
    a. store   b. student   c. study   d. shopper   e. cheer

21. **fan** ⟶ **cool : furnace** ⟶
    a. clean   b. stove   c. fuel   d. aggravate   e. heat

22. **fish** ⟶ **ocean : camel** ⟶
    a. pond   b. trees   c. desert   d. farm   e. pet

23. **son** ⟶ **father : father** ⟶
    a. family   b. grandfather c. man   d. mother   e. son

24. **soccer** ⟶ **sport : painting** ⟶
    a. sculpture   b. colors   c. game   d. art   e. clay

25. **button** ⟶ **coat : lock** ⟶
    a. pants   b. winter   c. door   d. bike   e. snap

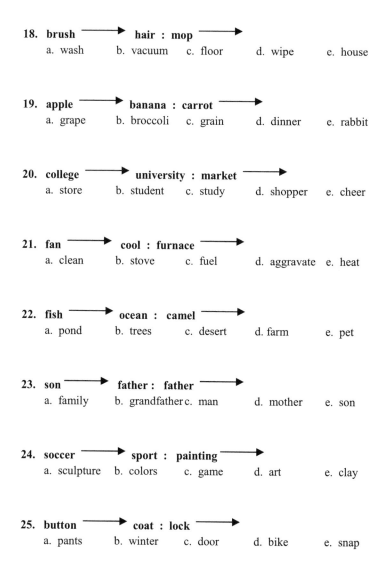

QUANTITATIVE RELATIONS

Each question in this section contains two items to compare. Review items I and II. Determine if one is greater than the other or if they are equal. Then select the answer that reflects that relationship.

25 questions
Approximate time to complete: 8 minutes

1. I. $0 + 4$
    II. $4 + 0$

    A. I is greater than II.
    B. I is less than II.
    C. I is equal to II.

2. I. $2 + 1 + 1$
    II. $1 + 2 + 2$

    A. I is greater than II.
    B. I is less than II.
    C. I is equal to II.

3.

    I   II

    A. I has more sides than II.
    B. I has fewer sides than II.
    C. I has the same number of sides as II.

4. I.   1 month
    II. 6 weeks

    A. I is a longer time than II.
    B. I is a shorter time than II.
    C. I the same length of time as II.

5. I. 4×1
    II. $1 + 1 + 1 + 1$

    A. I is greater than II.
    B. I is less than II.
    C. I is equal to II.

6. I.   10
    II. $10 + 0$

    A. I is greater than II.
    B. I is less than II.
    C. I is equal to II.

7. I.   11 - 4 - 5
    II. 4

    A. I is greater than II.
    B. I is less than II.
    C. I is equal to II.

8. I.   0 + 0 + 2
    II. 2 – 0 – 0

    A. I is greater than II.
    B. I is less than II.
    C. I is equal to II.

9. I.   300
    II. 030

    A. I is greater than II.
    B. I is less than II.
    C. I is equal to II.

10. I.   11 - 11
    II. 1 + 1

    A. I is greater than II.
    B. I is less than II.
    C. I is equal to II.

11. I.   20 minutes + 10 minutes
    II. 40 minutes

    A. I is greater than II.
    B. I is less than II.
    C. I is equal to II.

12. I.   1040
    II. 1004

    A. I is greater than II.
    B. I is less than II.
    C. I is equal to II.

13.

    I   II

    A. I has more sides than II.
    B. I has fewer sides than II.
    C. I has the same number of sides as II.

14. I.   10 – 5 + 5
    II. 5 + 5 - 10

    A. I is greater than II.
    B. I is less than II.
    C. I is equal to II.

15. I.   1 hour   A. I is greater than II.
  II. 65 minutes   B. I is less than II.
           C. I is equal to II.

16. I. $9 + 9 + 0$ A. I is greater than II.
  II. $10 + 9$ B. I is less than II.
           C. I is equal to II.

17. I.   2 nickels   A. I is more than II.
  II. 11 cents   B. I is less than II.
           C. I is equal to II.

18. I. $2 + 4 + 6$ A. I is greater than II.
  II. $4 + 6 + 0$ B. I is less than II.
           C. I is equal to II.

19. I.   2 boys + 1 girl A. I is more people than II.
  II. 1 boy + 3 girls B. I is less people than II.
           C. I has the same number of people
             as II.

20. I. $8 + 8 - 8$ A. I is greater than II.
  II. $10 - 10 + 10$ B. I is less than II.
           C. I is equal to II.

21. I.   30 minutes   A. I is a longer time than II.
  II. 1 hour   B. I is a shorter time than II.
           C. I the same length of time as II.

22. I. $400 + 20$ A. I is greater than II.
  II. $20 + 40$ B. I is less than II.
           C. I is equal to II.

23. I. 9 minutes + 11 minutes   A. I is greater than II.
    II. 12 minutes + 8 minutes   B. I is less than II.
                                    C. I is equal to II.

24. I. 80 cents   A. I is more than II.
    II. 3 quarters   B. I is less than II.
                                    C. I is equal to II.

25. I. 1201   A. I is greater than II.
    II. 1021   B. I is less than II.
                                    C. I is equal to II.

NUMBER SERIES

Each question in this section contains a series of numbers in bold. Review the numbers to determine the rule for their order. Select the number from the five available answers that should come next in the series.

20 questions
Approximate time to complete: 10 minutes

1. **1 2 3 4 5**   ⟶

    a. 4   b. 5   c. 6   d. 7   e. 8

2. **2 4 6 8 10**   ⟶

    a. 10   b. 11   c. 12   d. 13   e. 14

3. **19 18 17 16 15**   ⟶

    a. 10   b. 11   c. 12   d. 13   e. 14

4. **10 15 20 25 30**   ⟶

    a. 32   b. 35   c. 37   d. 40   e. 45

5. **22 24 26 28 30**   ⟶

    a. 31   b. 32   c. 34   d. 36   e. 38

6. **5 3 1 5 3 1**   ⟶

    a. 1   b. 2   c. 3   d. 5   e. 7

7. **3 5 7 9 11**   ⟶

    a. 10   b. 12   c. 13   d. 14   e. 15

8. **1   1   3   3   5   5 ⟶**
   a. 5   b. 6   c. 7   d. 10   e. 11

9. **100   90   80   70   60 ⟶**
   a. 30   b. 40   c. 50   d. 60   e. 70

10. $\frac{1}{1}$ $\frac{1}{2}$ $\frac{1}{3}$ $\frac{1}{4}$ $\frac{1}{5}$ ⟶
    a. $\frac{1}{7}$ b. $\frac{1}{6}$ c. $\frac{1}{5}$ d. $\frac{2}{5}$ e. $\frac{2}{7}$

11. **5   10   15   20   25 ⟶**
    a. 20   b. 25   c. 30   d. 35   e. 40

12. **5   7   9   11   13 ⟶**
    a. 12   b. 13   c. 14   d. 15   e. 16

13. **500   400   300   200   100 ⟶**
    a. 0   b. 10   c. 100   d. 150   e. 200

14. **9   9   11   11   13   13 ⟶**
    a. 13   b. 14   c. 15   d. 16   e. 17

15. $\frac{1}{8}$ $\frac{2}{8}$ $\frac{3}{8}$ $\frac{4}{8}$ ⟶
    a. 5   b. 8   c. $\frac{3}{4}$ d. $\frac{4}{7}$ e. $\frac{5}{8}$

16. **120   140   160   180 ⟶**
    a. 180   b. 190   c. 200   d. 210   e. 220

17. **99   97   95   93   91** ————▶

    a. 91   b. 90   c. 89   d. 87   e. 86

18. **17   27   37   47** ————▶

    a. 45   b. 50   c. 55   d. 52   e. 57

19. **9   9   8   8   7** ————▶

    a. 9   b. 8   c. 7   d. 6   e. 5

20. **1   2   4   7   11** ————▶

    a. 13   b. 14   c. 15   d. 16   e. 17

EQUATION BUILDING

Each question in this section contains a series of numbers and numerical signs in bold. Arrange and rearrange each of the numbers and signs to come up with one of the five available answers.

15 questions
Approximate time to complete: 12 minutes

1.   **1 2 3 + +**
      a. 4   b. 5   c. 6   d. 7   e. 8

2.   **1 2 4 + -**
      a. 1   b. 4   c. 5   d. 7   e. 9

3.   **2 7 9 + -**
      a. 1   b. 4   c. 9   d. 13   e. 16

4.   **1 6 9 - -**
      a. 2   b. 4   c. 9   d. 14   e. 16

5.   **1 2 5 + x**
      a. 6   b. 8   c. 9   d. 11   e. 14

6.   **3 4 12 + -**
      a. 5   b. 10   c. 13   d. 19   e. 21

7.   **5 5 6 + -**
      a. 0   b. 2   c. 5   d. 6   e. 8

8.   **6 8 10 + +**
      a. 12   b. 16   c. 18   d. 20   e. 24

9.   **3 6 9 - x**
    a. 9   b. 15   c. 16   d. 18   e. 20

10.   **2 4 8 16 - - -**
    a. 0   b. 2   c. 8   d. 24   e. 30

11.   **1 1 2 3 + + x**
    a. 5   b. 7   c. 8   d. 9   e. 10

12.   **2 3 4 x -**
    a. 3   b. 4   c. 6   d. 8   e. 10

13.   **7 8 9 9 + - -**
    a. 0   b. 3   c. 5   d. 18   e. 33

14.   **3 5 6 - x**
    a. 8   b. 13   c. 15   d. 21   e. 25

15. **1 4 5 x x**
    a. 10   b. 15   c. 20   d. 21   e. 25

FIGURE CLASSIFICATION

Review the first three figures in each question and determine why they are
similar. Select the figure from the five available answers that is most similar to
the first three figures.

25 questions
Approximate time to complete: 10 minutes

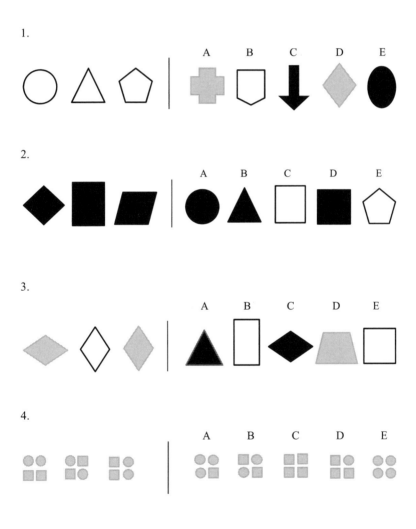

5.

6.

7.

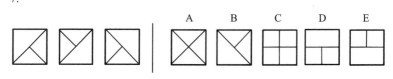

8.

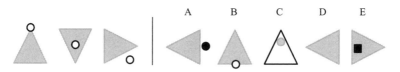

9.

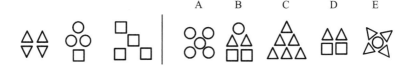

10.

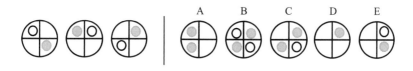

11.

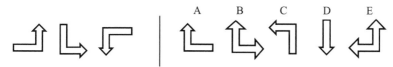

12.

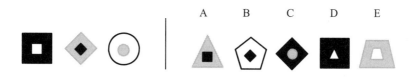

13.

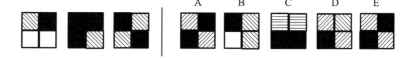

14.

15.

                              A   B   C   D   E

16.

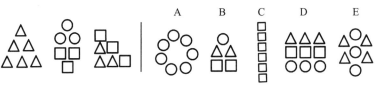

17.

18.

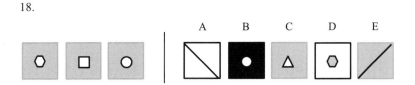

19.

20.

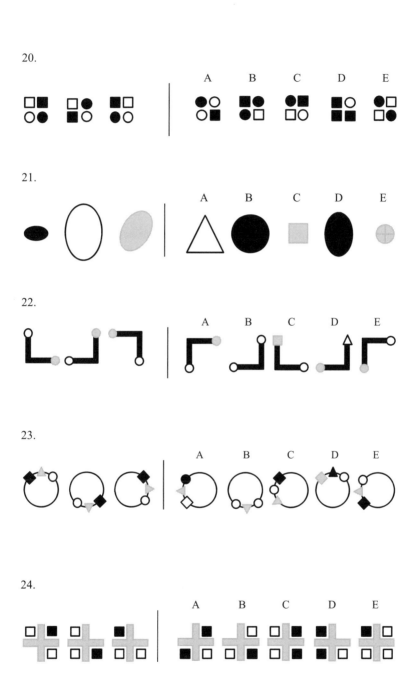

21.

22.

23.

24.

25.

FIGURE ANALOGIES

Review the first two figures in each question. The first figure is modified into
the second figure in some way.   Select the figure from the five available
answers that will be created when that same modification is done to the third
figure.

25 questions
Approximate time to complete: 10 minutes

1.

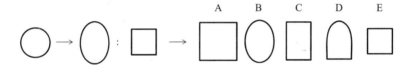

2.

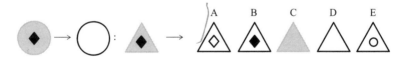

3.

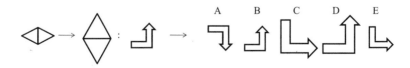

4.

5.

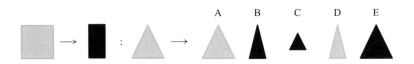

6.

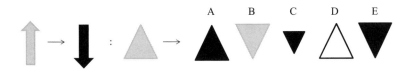

7.

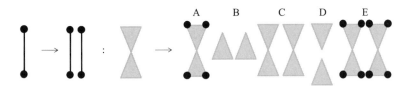

8.

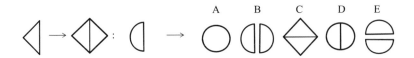

9.

10.

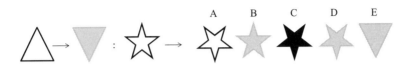

11.

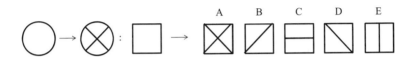

12.

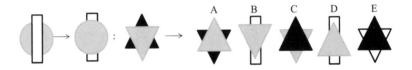

13.

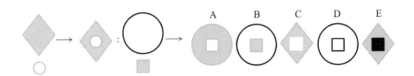

14.

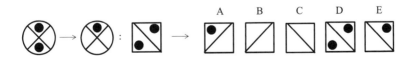

15.

16.

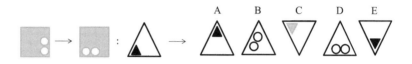

17.

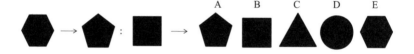

18.

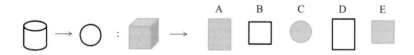

19.

20.

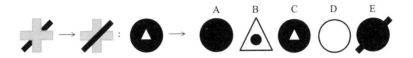

21.

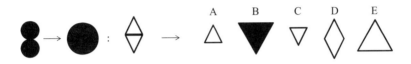

22.

23.

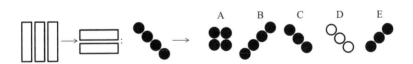

24.

25.

FIGURE ANALYSIS

Each question in this section shows a square piece of paper being folded and then hole-punched. Select the piece of paper from the five available answers that shows how the paper will look when it is unfolded.

15 questions
Approximate time to complete: 10 minutes

1.

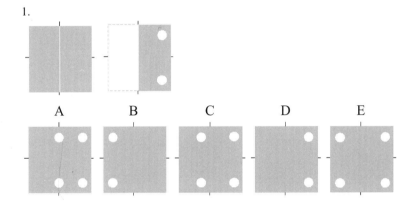

2.

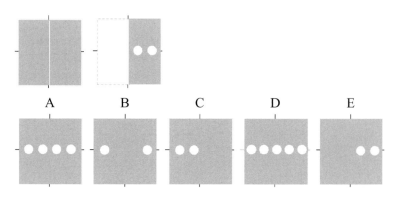

A   B   C   D   E

3.

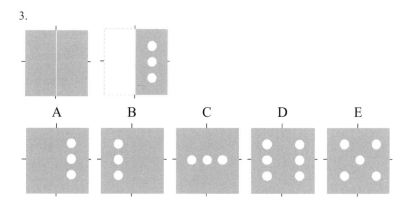

A   B   C   D   E

4.

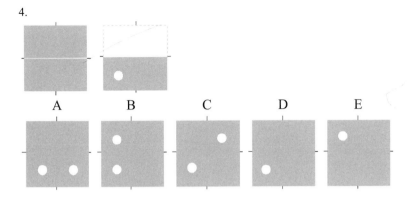

A   B   C   D   E

5.

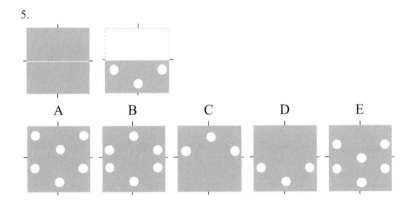

A   B   C   D   E

6.

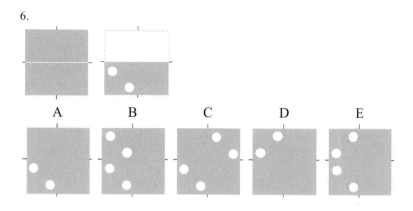

A   B   C   D   E

7.

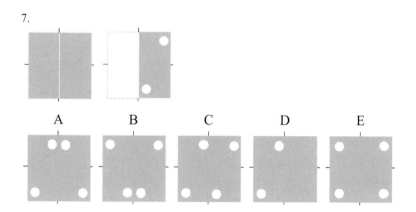

A   B   C   D   E

8.

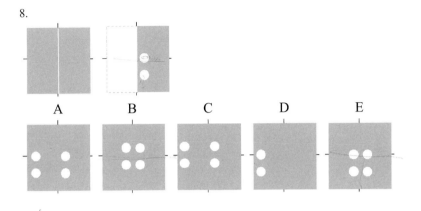

A   B   C   D   E

9.

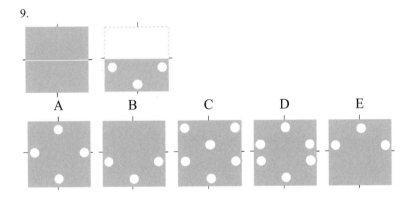

A   B   C   D   E

10.

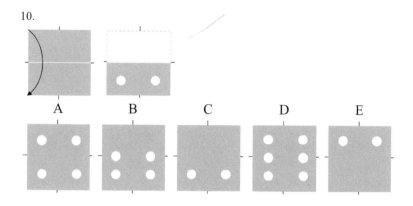

11.

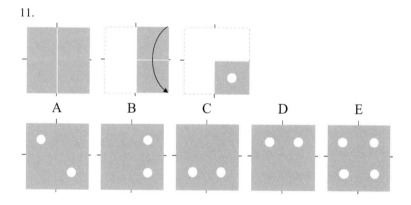

12.

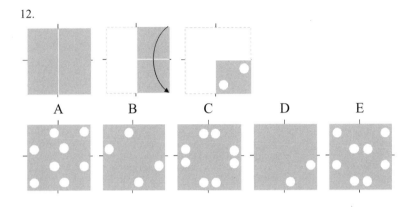

13.

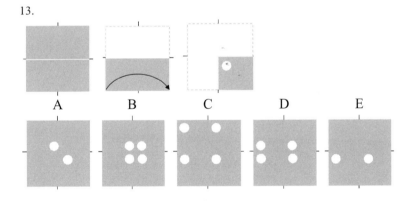

14.

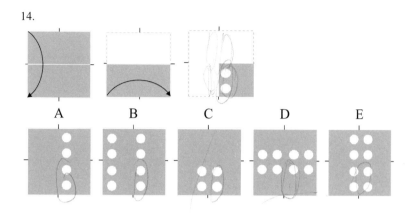

15.

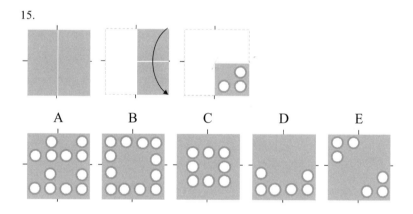

ANSWERS

VERBAL CLASSIFICATION

1. B
2. A
3. D
4. A
5. E
6. C
7. E
8. B
9. B
10. D
11. A
12. D
13. B
14. A
15. A
16. C
17. C
18. B
19. A
20. C

SENTENCE COMPLETION

1. B
2. C
3. E
4. B
5. C
6. B
7. A
8. C
9. B
10. E
11. C
12. A
13. D
14. B
15. E
16. C
17. B
18. C
19. E
20. D

VERBAL ANALOGIES

1. B
2. D
3. E
4. B
5. B
6. E
7. A
8. B
9. D
10. B
11. E
12. D
13. E
14. A
15. C
16. E
17. B
18. C
19. B
20. A
21. E
22. C
23. B
24. D
25. C

QUANTITATIVE RELATIONS

1. C
2. B
3. A
4. B
5. C
6. C
7. B
8. C
9. A
10. B
11. B
12. A
13. A
14. A
15. B
16. B
17. B
18. A
19. B
20. B
21. B
22. A
23. C
24. A
25. A

NUMBER SERIES

1. C
2. C
3. E
4. B
5. B
6. D
7. C
8. C
9. C
10. B
11. C
12. D
13. A
14. C
15. E
16. C
17. C
18. E
19. C
20. D

EQUATION BUILDING

1. C
2. C
3. B
4. A
5. D
6. C
7. D
8. E
9. A
10. B
11. C
12. E
13. B
14. B
15. C

FIGURE CLASSIFICATION

1. B
2. D
3. C
4. B
5. B
6. D
7. B
8. B
9. C
10. E
11. E
12. B
13. C
14. E
15. D
16. C
17. D
18. C
19. B
20. C
21. D
22. E
23. E
24. B
25. A

FIGURE ANALOGIES

1. B
2. C
3. D
4. C
5. B
6. E
7. E
8. C
9. D
10. D
11. A
12. C
13. B
14. E
15. A
16. A
17. C
18. E
19. C
20. A
21. E
22. C
23. E
24. E
25. A

FIGURE ANALYSIS

1. E
2. A
3. D
4. B
5. B
6. E
7. B
8. E
9. D
10. A
11. E
12. C
13. B
14. E
15. B

APPENDIX A

BUBBLE TEST FORM

Many errors are made on the CogAT®* exam because the students do not know how to fill out a bubble test form. Have your child practice filling in answers in the bubbles below.

1	Ⓐ Ⓑ Ⓒ Ⓓ Ⓔ					1	Ⓐ Ⓑ Ⓒ Ⓓ Ⓔ			
2	Ⓐ Ⓑ Ⓒ Ⓓ Ⓔ					2	Ⓐ Ⓑ Ⓒ Ⓓ Ⓔ			
3	Ⓐ Ⓑ Ⓒ Ⓓ Ⓔ					3	Ⓐ Ⓑ Ⓒ Ⓓ Ⓔ			
4	Ⓐ Ⓑ Ⓒ Ⓓ Ⓔ					4	Ⓐ Ⓑ Ⓒ Ⓓ Ⓔ			
5	Ⓐ Ⓑ Ⓒ Ⓓ Ⓔ					5	Ⓐ Ⓑ Ⓒ Ⓓ Ⓔ			
6	Ⓐ Ⓑ Ⓒ Ⓓ Ⓔ					6	Ⓐ Ⓑ Ⓒ Ⓓ Ⓔ			
7	Ⓐ Ⓑ Ⓒ Ⓓ Ⓔ					7	Ⓐ Ⓑ Ⓒ Ⓓ Ⓔ			
8	Ⓐ Ⓑ Ⓒ Ⓓ Ⓔ					8	Ⓐ Ⓑ Ⓒ Ⓓ Ⓔ			
9	Ⓐ Ⓑ Ⓒ Ⓓ Ⓔ					9	Ⓐ Ⓑ Ⓒ Ⓓ Ⓔ			
10	Ⓐ Ⓑ Ⓒ Ⓓ Ⓔ					10	Ⓐ Ⓑ Ⓒ Ⓓ Ⓔ			
11	Ⓐ Ⓑ Ⓒ Ⓓ Ⓔ					11	Ⓐ Ⓑ Ⓒ Ⓓ Ⓔ			
12	Ⓐ Ⓑ Ⓒ Ⓓ Ⓔ					12	Ⓐ Ⓑ Ⓒ Ⓓ Ⓔ			
13	Ⓐ Ⓑ Ⓒ Ⓓ Ⓔ					13	Ⓐ Ⓑ Ⓒ Ⓓ Ⓔ			
14	Ⓐ Ⓑ Ⓒ Ⓓ Ⓔ					14	Ⓐ Ⓑ Ⓒ Ⓓ Ⓔ			
15	Ⓐ Ⓑ Ⓒ Ⓓ Ⓔ					15	Ⓐ Ⓑ Ⓒ Ⓓ Ⓔ			
16	Ⓐ Ⓑ Ⓒ Ⓓ Ⓔ					16	Ⓐ Ⓑ Ⓒ Ⓓ Ⓔ			
17	Ⓐ Ⓑ Ⓒ Ⓓ Ⓔ					17	Ⓐ Ⓑ Ⓒ Ⓓ Ⓔ			
18	Ⓐ Ⓑ Ⓒ Ⓓ Ⓔ					18	Ⓐ Ⓑ Ⓒ Ⓓ Ⓔ			
19	Ⓐ Ⓑ Ⓒ Ⓓ Ⓔ					19	Ⓐ Ⓑ Ⓒ Ⓓ Ⓔ			
20	Ⓐ Ⓑ Ⓒ Ⓓ Ⓔ					20	Ⓐ Ⓑ Ⓒ Ⓓ Ⓔ			
21	Ⓐ Ⓑ Ⓒ Ⓓ Ⓔ					21	Ⓐ Ⓑ Ⓒ Ⓓ Ⓔ			
22	Ⓐ Ⓑ Ⓒ Ⓓ Ⓔ					22	Ⓐ Ⓑ Ⓒ Ⓓ Ⓔ			
23	Ⓐ Ⓑ Ⓒ Ⓓ Ⓔ					23	Ⓐ Ⓑ Ⓒ Ⓓ Ⓔ			
24	Ⓐ Ⓑ Ⓒ Ⓓ Ⓔ					24	Ⓐ Ⓑ Ⓒ Ⓓ Ⓔ			
25	Ⓐ Ⓑ Ⓒ Ⓓ Ⓔ					25	Ⓐ Ⓑ Ⓒ Ⓓ Ⓔ			

NOTES

NOTES